Space Cowboys

how i learned to ignore the ticking and love the bomb

a collection of poetry

by

Agnew T. (Goldwater) Pickens

cover art by

Patricia Anne Donohue

Burnt Hamster Publishing
Copyright 2011

Introduction

I wrote these poems from November 1, 2009 until today, December 15, 2011. This volume of poetry starts with the experimental poem *Space Christals* and ends with *How I Learned to Ignore the Ticking and Love the Bomb*, hence the title of this volume of poetry. Usually, the poems are a journal of my life in Ohio and California and are presented pretty much in order of being written. I wrote well over 400 poems during this period and am presenting what I feel are my best or most important poems. Space Christals is posted with some commentary.

I am thankful for all my wonderful teachers, living and dead, and wish to specifically thank Joan Krejcar, who taught me the Alla Prima method in oil painting which I applied to the vast majority of these poems. Also, I would like to thank Corey D Cleven, who involved me in the Remix Experiment Project back in 2008.

I hope that you enjoy reading these poems as much as I enjoyed writing them.

Agnew T. (Goldwater) Pickens

for my beloved Jianna

**Poems and Work
written in Ohio
November 1, 2009
to March 7,
2010**

5Pac3 ChrisTa15

On CrY-5t.MaSS mOrn1nG

DaV1D cOm3s WaGginG 4Cro5s
to eAt tEh SpAc3 PumPk1n Ba1t

A5 1 Mine 5yNtHeTiC B4cT3riA Chr15tals
iN mY PsyCh3deLiC 5Pac3 Su1t

F0r a s1M(u)l4T3d 5aNtA C14Us
bl0wIng bAgP1p3s aT 5 AM

On Teh DarK s1De of sUnSpoT
24/7/11/365.

PaR4D153 l2 is aWfU11y C0ld
wiThout t3H BurNinG f05-S0(u)L5

La t3a Da

OH Shit!

T3h c4NdY bAr mAch1ne
in t3h 5paCe f1ll1Ng staTi0n

1s oN Teh FriTz AG41N!

CoNteXt(u)a1itY qU3U3es aBounD
tEh LiMiTs Of T3H 1MagInAt1iON.

gAwd i5 0n Su1CiDe W4tcH
f0r teH 1aSt RuN oF tEh DaY

M0tH3r dE4Th is F3cuNd W1tH Po5siBb1liTieS BTW

Spr1nkLe m0r3 All4H ChR15tals
 On teh C0rNf1ak3s on teh Fr0nT14wN.

t3h VaCuUM ha5 a CraCk 1n iT AgAin

1t f3elS jU5t 1ikE a Tr4CtoR tRa1l0r
 ruNninG tHro(u)gH y0uR h3aD.

1eT uS M4k3 tIme t0 aPp14Ud teh S0uNd
 oF d1St4nT g(un)Fir3 1n TeH CaTh3(t3r)dR4l

d1nG D0Ng
 L3t tH3rE bE Pe4S 0n 3aRtH!
DiNg donG!
 leT TheR3 B3 p3as oN e4rTh
dInG DonG!
 13t tHER3 b3 P34S 0N 34RTH!

FI-NI-TE!

Transcription and commentary

Space Christals

on christmas morning

David comes wagging across
to eat the space Pumpkin bait

(David is a Golden retriever that lives
across the street & Pumpkin is a cat)

*as i mine synthetic bacteria christals
in my psychedelic space suit*

*for a simulated Santa Claus
blowing bagpipes at 5 AM*

*(flashback memory of a bagpiper on the streets
of New York City who i dropped $5 to 17 years ago)*

*on the darkside of sunspot
24/7/11/365*

*(i imagine that their are beings who regularly harvest
synthetic bacteria christals behind sunspots)*

*Paradise 12 is awfully cold
without the burning fossils(souls)*

la ti da

*oh shit!
the candy bar machine
in the space filling station*

is on the fritz again!

*(returning from the sunspot with synthetic bacteria
for the home planet, i make my usual stop to refuel and
snack)*

*contextuality queues abound
the limits of the imagination*

(c.f. contextuality cues in linguistics)

*God is on suicide watch
for the last run of the day*

Mother Death is fecund with possibilities by the way

*sprinkle more Allah christals
on the cornflakes on the front lawn*

*(i see ice cubes poured in the grass of a fast food restaurant
and imagine them to be Allah crystals)*

the vacuum has a crack in it again

*it feels just like a tractor trailer
running through your head*

*let us make time to applaud
the sound of distant gunfire in the cathe(ter)dral*

*ding dong!
let there be peas(peace) on Earth*

*ding dong!
let there be peas on Earth*

*ding dong!
let there be peas on Earth*

fi-ni-te

The Bread Is Risen

*The Bread is risen
  on the observation deck
    of our little station of the Crossroad*

*Just in time for
  the transmigration of the fowl
    to their summer palaces.*

*I'm catching a few H. Ray's
  out on the solar panels
    in the heat of the blinding Moon.*

*Don't sweat the delivery,
  just open wide and receive
    your hosts with Earthly delight!*

*The cran-grape juice is excellent
  with the risen Bread and
    makes a Steamed Hamster*

*As happy as a Baby Carrot
  to wallow with the swine-flu
    in the comfort of an epidemic.*

Can't you taste the Bread is Risen?

Behind The Monolith

*Behind the Monolith is
 a hand-scribbled note*

On the back of a drugstore receipt.

"I could still see you"

*when your face shattered
 at the news of the departure...*

*Lying in a heap of other notes,
 some just as incongruous with the*

Continuous hum of the MonOLith.

*Here's one:
"Bacon
Chloroform
Map of Berlin 2006"
written on a cocktail napkin
in lipstick.*

Means nothing to me.

*So I search through the scraps
 that lie at my feet for what seems like-*

And then I find it.

*Written in my hand on
a used bus ticket from the future*

"It isn't so"

underneath an orange sky

the pocket krakatoas are working overtime
filling the air with sulfuric hilarity
on board the mother planet i call home
tanning carrots underneath an orange sky

shed a tear

shed a tear for Jed McGrady
he thought he found himself a lady
he bought himself a brand new suit
they buried him in it with his boots

his name is b.

i meet him by the ashcan, his name is b.
he's a poet like i someday dream to be

i've known him at the center where i get
my anti-insanity inoculations every two weeks

he shows me his latest poem, it's called:
"I am not a Schizophrenic any more"

i love his fantastic psychedelic handwriting
he says he might write some poetry about horses
all i know about horses
is not to bet on them like my dad did

b. is a great guy
he has so many friends
he sometimes forgets my name
if he doesn't see me for a couple months
but he remembers my name this time

he never forgets my face
he always smiles at me when he sees me
he likes to smoke out by the ashcan
and suffers the happy idiot a glimpse

Cork!

Cork built him some arches
  for all the boeuf junkies

who even now

Line up at his golden gates
  for what sure tastes like

SALIVATION!

I can see the double rainbow
  at the foot of Orion's Belt.

SALISBURY STEAK!

should have it

SO GOOD!

Whatever you do don't

Order the SURPRISE MEAL!

Cerberus with his transplanted heads
  and I'm sure he tastes nothing

at all like baby carrots!

Though I didn't take a nibble.

He was so cute all I wanted

to do list:

1) take him home with me!
2) feed him baby carrots!
3) pet him like a lover!

SALVATION!

beacon hum

*beacon hum bouncing signal off the left antenna shut
your yawning refrigerator door the cheese works round
the mousetrap enema ejector shield cable box splitter
pea soup and nuts bolt through my neck daddy-O flips a
frisbee golf cart before the horse crosses himself in front of the
finish your broccoli spears if you seek amiable tears
before freezing rain in the forecastle and hounds zounds and
out of boundary roundelay jones approving
the last breath of winter of our disco blister prick your finger
make the packed lunch for two sod hoppers
to notice the beacon hum*

Be(tween) The Clock And The Bed

The slumber alarm alert
rouses you from your reverie...
ticking, ever ticking - until the power fails!

The springs in the mattress
poke and prod you in your sleep,
is this any way to construct a dream loop?

The dig(i)tal flashes lotto results
through the veil of darkness:
always off by one /error/ no results returned.

The tooth fairy leaves a bullet under your pillow.
Will you have your head examined in the morning?
There is no rest for the wicked so(u)l
be(tween) the clock and the bed.

(Standing In Line) At The Pay Confessional

(Standing in line) at the pay confessional
in my photo opportunity suit,
a cabaret of poetry in one hand,
just currency for some canceled Czech,
I get to the magic number dispenser lotto machine
but it's empty!

A mime in drag with a roll of ticker tapes
sidles up to the promontory of the receiving unit
with the Host.

Will I get to taste Sal(i)vation or have to settle
for Sal(i)sbury Steak instead. Damned mystery meat plagues
my dentifricial overtures!

I take a numberless number, it's best not to look.
I will be called to the hot seat when my time is /UP/!

Scenic variations drift through my view-strator as I... i.. i.

(stand) in line waiting at the pay confessional.

liquid butterfly christals

*soon the moon-singing beetles will be
spraying liquid butterfly christals
across the prairies of your consciousness
with flapping wings in harmonies
unheard by human heresies and
hysterical raptures will ensue*

*short order cooks will stop to feed the Sun
craps tables will get stuck in seven/eleven
cars won't know which way to turn or when to run
by commandment of the Mother, Earth unto Heaven*

*rhymes will spontaneously diverge
unknown poets will emerge*

songs unsung will find their voices

*suffer the Children
suffer the Chosen
suffer no more
the mirror frozen*

*what are the choices?
what are the options?
red pill, blue pill?
some say there's a third pill
i've heard it comes in purple*

*hmm wonder what it does...
look inside the medicine cabinet
i think you might find your prescription
has already been filled*

all it takes is one

*i'm already there
come join the fun
the Party has begun*

Sal(i)vatio

I'm not a pusher
so I'm leaving the envelopes at home.

I'm taking the scenic route
to sen(i)lity, sal(i)vation and sal(i)nity.
Take my advice and avoid the cutoff

from familiar things and friends
and long-forgotten memories.

You'll be better off left to your own devices!

Let Your Spirit that dwells within You
Be Your Guide.

Now /off/

the purple pill of madness

*in a thousand years
in some ecstatic frenzy
i may go mad beyond recovery
and wander off across the milky way
to sit upon a speck of dust
and ponder a coke booger
i once drew
from my left nostril*

*you may not be so fortunate
when you see the light of error
retrieval is for dog stars*

*see me madly laughing
at everything you hold dear*

*you will have plenty
to laugh about plenty
to think you could have
once looked a melting gaze
upon your adversary*

*now your latitude is platitudes
and your beattitudes are flatulence*

*you took the purple pill of madness
it's too beautiful*

*i know
it's true
i took it too*

you will have everything you desire
and more than you desire
and nothing you desire
will come as a surprise

but it needn't be this way
you can dream your cares away
to your heart's desire
come and sit by the fire
madness is a fine state of loving
the creative will is yours

The Fugitive

On their first meeting,
  the Fugitive comes to the
    Adversary's front door
But the Fugitive isn't there.

On their second meeting,
  the Adversary comes to the
    Fugitive's front porch
And leaves the Adversary his Staff.

The Fugitive and the Adversary never meet.

Again

Zion

*Riding the main road into Zion,
daydreaming
of the Pope
taking off his miter
and jacking off to a picture
of Gertrude Stein and Alice B. Toklas
doing it on a divan,*

*Riding,
sweat dripping from my mustache,
it tastes like your sex
and I'm thinking of you,
far away in Zion,
lying in bed
with a dyke named Hal
eating Malomars and smoking Pall Malls,
Malomar crumbs on your saggy, brown belly.*

*I'll be in Zion in 12 and a half hours
if I push the Dodge the rest of the ride
and don't get stopped for speeding.
Can I have coffee with you in the morning?
Will you let me tell you dirty stories
while I make you scream?*

*Tell Hal to put your key under the mat
when she leaves.
I have a trunk full of Malomars.*

sal(i)vation bell

*going to the walmart to cash my inability check
on a winter's day
i stop like one of pavlov's dogs by the sal(i)vation bell*

*yeah i saw their ads on television
where i could extract the lucre
it's for a good cause and ringing the bell
for an hour in the cold
would do me good or so i thought*

*so i ask the man:
"can i ring the bell?"*

*he says his manager will be back in twenty minutes
i can ask him
so i go inside to extract the lucre
from my inability check
and maybe feed a little bit to the sal(i)vation bell people.*

*my head is humming
at the thought of all the cold hard cash
pouring in the pot
as i stand in line at the service bay
thinking about ringing the bell*

*it's for a good cause and
ringing the bell for an hour in the cold
would do me good
so i collect my lucre and go outside
to ask the man
and when i get to the sal(i)vation bell
the manager is emptying the pot
so i ask the man:
"can i ring the bell?"*

and he says:
"you'll have to go downtown and fill out an application"

hmmm

what do i look like? look at me
one of pavlov's hungry dogs
who wants just once to ring the bell
and they want me to fill out an application
to stand out in the cold
ringing the sal(i)vation bell
and i look like the guy who ate the receipts
but i'm not
and i thank the man and drop a jackson into the bucket
and wonder what has become of me

untitled 5

the reverend right beagle sings his hymn
a whim to thin the din of pan's fluting melody on high
as i turn my gaze unto the sky
* and wonder why*

the cycle seems so refreshing
in the gleam of the scimitar
a bridge too far for broken dreams

and moonbeam mcsway is on the way
to better things of hearts and springs
welling up into eternities
that if you please me
i will turn the burning bush
into a kafka breath of everfresh lullabies
as she sighs the longing breath
until the death of mourning doves
on winsome loves
cast in lurid colors

'tis of thee
the wheel has gotten spoken
and the echo returns unbroken
on the wind of triumphs yet unclaimed by vagrant wastrels
on the alleyways the minstrel plays the tune
unto the tide of tillage spilled
upon the landscape of forever days

a valentine massacre

*meet me if you dare
in the cartage company
where i can line you up
against a bare cement wall

and spray you with
toasted strawberry kiss gunfire
and spray your blood

against my wishes
against my ecstasies
against my desire

you won't suspect a thing
when i show up
in my uniform existence
that i carted out of a violin case
holding a sub-machine gun heart

against your will?
against all hope?
against all odds!

ah, go quietly dove
it won't hurt a bit

and the papers will say
i did it all for love*

Program Wobbly

111 feeling a bit wobbly-wobbly '(?)'
112 gotta lay off the hallucinogenic poetry for a while
113 this hell of laughter mirth and merriment is making me dizzy
114 how do you get /off/ this thang '(?)'
115 when do you get /off/ '(?)'
121 wanna come over and smoke some cigs eat cheese and drink some whiskey til we puke '(?)'
122 i m getting me-sick
123 i m getting home-sick
124 i m getting poem-sick
125 somebody call my mama cause i need a new set of snow tires for the minivan
131 BLUE MOON
132 how do y all do this without fist-fucking the computer '(?)'
133 my mouse my mouse my mouse is on a wire '(!)'
134 for the love of Hitler will you please tell me where the /off/ button is '(?)'
135 wipe that shit-eating grin off your face if you re not gonna share '(!)'
141 i ve come to a decision
142 i like you '(!)'
143 that s why i m going to shut the fuck up '(!)'
144 feeling a bit wobbly-wobbly '(!)'
145 END

If I Could

if i could stand on my tippy toes
 on the edge of my universe to touch

touch
touch
that hollow place inside you where

only you feel alone.

what's the point?

if i could i would tell you that

it's alright to feel alone inside your head.

alone inside the vastness you were meant to be.

what's the point?

so that you could stand on your tippy toes
 on the edge of your universe to touch

touch
touch
that hollow place inside me that
only you can fill.

The Seventh Seal

*The wizard takes the sacred book
from its protective sleeve.*

*The Space Ghost battles divers
Space Demons on its hallowed cover.*

cross yourself 3X

The wizard opens the book to page 85 (unmarked).

*There is an illustration showing a dark-haired mustached man
facing Space Ghost and the caption at the bottom reads:*

"A Uniformed Official Greets Space Ghost"

aside- is that an uninformed official?

There will be no spell cast at this juncture by the wizard.

Cross Yourself 3X

Alpha Omega

command sequence

<copy> this /off/ the SCREAM
at the <break> of the <space> ~bar~
the doors and <lock> the demons /on/
the <key> boarding PASS/FAIL systems
that <login> only to Abort? Retry?
...leave the keyboard to its terminal flight:
breathe, breathe in the air and feel the mystery
and dream to unravel it.
dare, dare to look around at what you have wrought.
you are the master of the command sequence.

the h(a)unting ground

you have journeyed far
many friends you have
left behind along the way
the h(a)unting ground lies near
when you reach it they will know

My (Last) Oil Change <end game>

square nine opens up
along the corridors of portent

they put the minivan on the rack
for a quick peek

rogues and beggars line up
with hugs and kisses
to stake their claim

about two quarts low and
needs a new oil filter

but i'll take the fugitive
to block
the grid is opening
up to another square

they lube her up and
refill the wiper fluid
so what's the twisting point?
another game>? <end it already

as i drive away
another satisfied customer

heaven?

*mother teresa is pushing
a shopping cart filled with
potatoes and toaster ovens
along the alley ways
of a ghetto on the outskirts
of the shining city
while saddam sits in council
with seven virgins lying naked,
their skin gleaning energy
from the Son,
beside the swimming lagoon
in a sleepy suburb,
gleaming towers in their view.
love radiates from the Center
directed outwards,
the devotion of Love's children
directs it inwards.
the heart of the city beats
like a drummer's orgasmic solo,
the rhythm is there,
can you feel the beat?
you can't beat the feel
of the Creator's will
etched upon the footprints
in the wheelhouse of your mind.
Heaven is but a breath away,
do you dare to draw it in?*

Poems and Lyrics
Written in California
March 2010 to July 2011

bubonic playground

*at the dawn of the beginning
of what never ends,
going 'round, bringing out the dead,*

*shall we feast upon the corpses
of those we've hated and loved?
or laugh and lament over their withering bones?*

*on the bubonic playground that we share,
don't shed a tear for oilspills or bloodspills.*

*let's all scream our heads together
for the love that's been spilled
like empty seed on barren ground.*

*let's all scream our faces in the mirror
until we melt together
and just for once leave hate and discontent behind.*

Note to Self #6

*my heart may skip a beat in rhythm
or even stop for a pause
but it will never stop loving you...*

*the god inside you
will lift you up
if you let her!*

*the gods are like
a pulsating massage shower
on your feet
all over your body
if it feels real...*

*L-O-V-E is the fertilizer
of your imagination
and barbecue is also a research poem!*

*i'm the LOUD p-e-a-c-e junkie
who stayed clean @)~
and i'm locked on maximum gratitude
at the moment.*

*stuff disappearing on the 'puter
only needs someone's magic imagination
R-E-S-T-o-r-a-t-i-o-n
with good friends
so see what happens!*

Fragment of a Sub(URBAN) Daydream

*Nirvana is a short NAP
in a BROOKlined cemetery...*

*Meanwhile,
there are memory bank rob(BERRIES) in progress
for the POOR concentration CAMPERS.*

*Everywhere the CLEAN streets are
lined with litter bins collecting DUST
particles along the BACK
of their Alley Ca(r)t-wheels...*

*can you spare A. Diamond
For a CUP of laughter in the park
as Shake-The-Speare wiggles a toe in the SAND?*

*(Definitely)
put the RUBY on Thursday's pulse
This TIME out
so you can meet at BO(o)TH ends
in the Middle sometimes
If oHIo calls again,*

*ears prick up your arse in UNI(S)ON
As you SURF the radio WAVES
for pent-up or strangled melodies...*

*Wait for it! just wait... remember, Milton,
your services have ALREADY been rendered
in your HOLIDAY pants
and SMILING is only your favorite Opt-i(o)n.*

an irregular Jesus

an irregular Jesus
who likes to take vacations in the asylum
walks into Ace hardware for some glass cleaner
and gets lost

he finds himself in line with a bottle of pneumonia
when the lady in front of him has her credit declined
and walks away empty handed

he yallers, "Hey! i got a GOLD tooth."
but she disapppears

he forgets his first miracle for a moment
and the pain in his chest nearly drops him to the floor

he laughs and waves at the security camera
remembering to wander
to the corner to clean a few windows for the Man

-The RELIEF Pitcher

DURING a simultaneous NAP exposure,
the poetic JUSTICE of the PIECES
collects the REWARD MAP.

Hunting TREASURES high and low,
his/her TOUCH reunites lost LOVERS
until they BUILD the broken MIRROR
SHUDDERING/shattering TOGETHER.

eventually NOW feels like PARADISE tomatoes
under cLOUDs of MUSH-room skies.
Onions shed a tear for HUMANITY
once held together by SPAGHETTI and HAPPY memories.

Happiness returns like the TIDE to THOSE
who remember how to FEEL their TOES
and GOD forbid they should find an extra
<ONE> under their PILLOW.
Remember, it's still in the UNDERWEAR drawer!

WHEN you find the shallows in the RIVER
with your feet, dive under and swim like a MINNOW
until the Tsunami carries you
to the OTHER side of WHERE you belong again.

Imagine another FUTURE
with everything that you have ever LOVED
and ROOM for love to GROW
like a ripe BABY
strawberry BUNNY in the Easter grass.

Love is an EASY habit to Mastery
and the joy of epinephrine PULSING through your body
refreshes your SOUL.
Flex the plexus solar SYSTEM into GENTLE winding bridges!
SUSPENSIONS/emulsions of non-belief
will provide the SPACE your napkin requires
for you to re-awaken KUNDALINI
if you try ANOTHER floppy-eared horse to LAND HOME.

s-a-f-e-t-y FIRST when you cross-TRUMP
station and look where you went behind
BREAD crumbs Hansel's regret
was leaving Gretel's SIDE to eat the GINGER bread.
Get baked with the WICKER witch
if that's what you really want
as CLARITY is an OBVIOUS CHOICE
for those who KNOW what they want.

L-O-V-E begets l-o-v-e and so does hatred
and what's the DIFFERENTIAL got to do with PACEM,
dona NOBIS fun FUN fun
until responsibilities WASH away 7 errors lost INSIDE
(made of reversible MATERIAL)
a WORD puzzle.
Shoeless Joe may say it isn't so
but love inbreeds the corruption
of a lost satellite's MASTER file adopted by the WINDS.
AGAIN when you get there NOW you will be THERE.

HAPPINESS for two is the SUPREME PIZZA.
HAPPINESS and JOY for ALL
is the SUPER s-u-p-r-e-m-e MUFFIN baker.

Do you remember when your ELBOW was an ASS-hole
to your MOM and DAD eventually?
Well it was all in their imagination.

Don't cry OUT! cry tears of liquid JOY
and PURPLE hamsters in their PAISLEY garb
as if they no longer prefer PLAID.

a CLASS of OTHER rodents
swing their CHARIOTS
toward a H-O-L-O-c-o-a-s-t-e-r/h-o-l-o-G-R-A-P-H
in zig-ZAG-gy SPIRALS,
emphasis added in between SIGHS/size.

REMEMBER, Pin-occhio was a MARION-ette
before he was a BOY or GIRL again.
WATCH how gracefully the HUM-mingbird offers itself
to the FLOWERS. in RETURN
the flow-ers give up,
NECTAR pouring from their SILK-en throats.

Once more, the TURKEY gathers with her FLOG/flock
and gobbles away the sadness of t-h-a-n-k-s-g-i-v-i-n-g
and joy AGAIN ensues.

Let yourself off the HOOK at any EXIT
and you will see FLORENCE, IT-ally in a happier TOMORROW.
now arrives soon
when you recall the SEARCH p-a-r-t-y
so don't hurt Tiresias' feelings in the MEAN-time/tide.
Ann Oracle speaks to SPARE before she strikes
but rolled a perfect GAME.
3X.
3 times in a ROW of cardboard HOUSES.

Powdered instant RECALL takes a w-h-i-l-e
to dis-SOLVE in a LTD
quantity of H20 and OLDS-mobiles are FOR/four PUSSYcats
so I will take my TOFU tenderloin MEDIUM rare.

The ICE CREAM trucks are double parked
and COLLECTING tickets in the RAIN.

It's OK to do a LITTLE damage
to your nervous TICKLE system once in a while,
just DON"T become a NUN/none in a habit/HOBBIT.
IF a train of THOUGHT derails you,
seek RELIEF in a COMEDY/accomodation of ROMANCE.
A. Bird will come along to give YOU a FEATHER
for your MATTRESSES
and your pillow will nap UNDER your HEAD.

ACCEPT/except responsibility to RESTORE GOOD FAITH
and you CAN CLIMB the highest MOUNTAIN
back to THE shoreline in a NATURAL CONTOUR recliner.
your TRUE lover may ENJOY a gentle FOOT massage
for A. Glimpse of ECSTASY
and a HEALTHY fear of gods OUTSIDE
can SPARK the IMAGINATION.
Your EYES/ayes MAY find BEAUTY where ugliness ONCE
reigned.

I would/WOOD give YOU my KIDNEY BEANS
as long as our TISSUES match
and REISSUE myself aNEW
SET MATCH-ing desires
with the GREAT DESIRE, LOVE.

time hangs ON the BALANCE BEAM
of insanity DEFENSE
and fences ONLY keep WORMS
from eating the DUST bunnies underneath your BED.
Whence, you FIND a happy castle,
help a MOTH-er OFF a WEB
so panic GRASS used to be.
What YOU and I have PUT/putt TOGETHER

let not gods plunder.
**WORSHIP the TEMPLE of your BODY when we MEET again.
LOOK at US NOW.**

Note to Self #8

love has no logic but the freedom of expression...

*does a book have dreams of taking naps
in a quiet library?
or being adapted/adopted in a book store?*

*or is an easily suggestible digestive system
good for the solar system?*

*I love the smell of napalm
on your pancakes or maybe
some nuclear/unclear maple syrup...*

*but Big Al drew a stinky
and the cyanitrous wouldn't feel good there
so Anna kindly gave me ten for nine
and rendered unto Ceasar Salad.*

*As a reconfigured veteran
of the psychic imagination game
i like to go where I can feel the love...*

*I do love zippers
on marshmallow pants
and sprinkling the bamboo jungle
in my friend's gardens
cause it smiles back with rainbows!*

a little doll with no name

Pink rosy cheeks
and orange ribbons in her brown hair...
accordion arms and legs

1972 Ideal Toy Corp.

given to me by my friend
but she isn't mine yet

she looks happy in her purple case
as a tear falls on the floor

all she has are the clothes on her back
and a pair of black boots I found walking
the Dead End
and they don't even fit her pretty feet

she brought joy once to a little girl
who took such good care of her
in the clapboard house she grew up in...

the little girl grew up and moved on
but the doll remains
and somehow I feel the Goddess Energy
when I look into the doll's eyes...

She belongs to someone who can imagine
and recharge the sparkle in her eyes.

I know she isn't real
but I love her still...

She deserves a Happy home
and the love a little girl can bring

*To be young again
and imagine the possibilities
when a dream opened a Door
to Future promises.*

nothing much happens on Tuesdays

*nothing much happens
on Tuesdays in Heaven,
or Hell
for that matter
you can dawdle
at the Pearly Whites
and ride the Tube through
Purgatorio...*

*nothing much happens
on Tuesdays on Earth,
or the Moon
would up and leave
its place in the sky
assured
that the distance
can always be crossed by Apollo...*

*nothing much happens
on Tuesdays except in my Heart,
or my Imagination
would run away with you
all over again
rapt
in your loving presence
that keeps the air pumping
in my Lungs.*

Uncle Pavlov's Bell

walking around the park,
up and down, round and around,
I smell the hungry sitting down

for hotdogs, the best,
for burritos, sushi, coffee,
all sorts of good stuff...

now I've just filled my belly
before coming to the park
but the smell of all this food
is making the lions in tummy growl!

i spent my last paper money
in the illusion arcade
so sitting at restaurant
is not an option.

my mind screams for ice cream!
i take a magic penny that I found
to the wishing waterfall rapids
and toss it in!

hmm, no ice cream... yet

i'm not hungry, i just wanted some
walking around the park,
and ice cream is good for a tricky knee
on a hot summer day,
walking around the park

as the meter running in my head
tells me it's time to go...

a napkin orphanage

*where the odd cloth napkins gather
in their tatters,
hopelessly mismatched,
two white napkins find each other
and enfold in embrace
like lost lovers.*

*everything has a soul
and even a cloth napkin
can yearn for its mate
and find someone to love
in a napkin orphanage*

even if its edges are frayed.

when poets run the world

when poets run the world as if they already don't
(but that's another subject entirely),
when poets run the world,
fractal rainbows appear by command performance
above white castles in the orange sky
and the throngs gather under the rainclouds
to celebrate in their mud dance huts
up to their elbows in a rugby scrum.

when poets run the world,
pavlov's bell will go unnoticed;
in fact the whole clock thing will appear
as the real illusion that it is.

when poets run the world
everybody's hands will be on their own switches,
forgetting the manipulations,
forgetting the machinations,
remembering the God nature within everybody's everyone,
everything will just be as the poet's dream.

when poets run the world as if they already don't
(but that is what the poets focus on),
when poets run the world,
the doors will open wide in a grand gesture bow
and everyone will rise up in song
at the festival of feasts and feats resumes
in memories of what dreams unfold.

when poets run the world,
the news gossip will comfort the masses
on this rollercoaster ride we call a planet;
like springboards, eyes will turn to possibilities
instead of eventualities and actuaries

*because the insurance man can go fuck himself,
a sparrow doesn't need a policy for its nest,
a sparrow builds to suit and dreams whatever
it wants into existence
and lest a sparrow fall was only an illusion
in the first damn place.*

*when poets run the world,
well you know what?
look around.*

life is a poem when poets run the world.

just another Thursday

*got to sleep in last night
and it felt so good...*

*took care of my bunk
in the spacely station
and brushed the cemetery
off in my mouth.*

*had some star clusters
for a fast break
and ventured from my capsule
for a downhill climb*

*to return
a little doll's black space boots
left on top of an email box...*

*the view on the holocoaster
was beautiful and refreshing
on this Thursday morning*

*and the variable gravity
of the situation
gave me a nice cardio-blast.*

*some bird from Toronto
is lecturing a squirrel
about maintaing a balanced diet*

*and I whistle at a Banana
Who whistles back in joy!*

Wicked Umbrellasphere

*Twisting like a wind-up clock rest,
a wandering umbrella greets*

*What?
is next to What?*

*greets a smiling Balloon/baboon
guided by a wishing Yokel*

*victorious nonetheless in an offhand weigh-in
as the Herald pays*

TRIBUTARY privilege to a greenleaf

*falling on a threadbare rug
covering and recovering What? Pax Humana
for a moment,
a glimpse of respite*

*from Spherical Oceans
dropping dripping dropping
patter pitter with the green leaves*

on a wicked Umbrella

Salamander Alley

a large green pepper (knowing right well)
mistakes Salamander Alley for a resting spot

and becomes ensnared
in a gravitational orbit tug-of-war
as all eyes

look like maypole adjectives
wriggling in streamatics
in the undercurrents of a fixation...

galaxies await the outcome
while whistling like lost teakettles
on the horizontal hold of a cracked universe.

black plumes are peppered with the drum
of a starring roll in fantastic ecstasies of what

to a casual onlooker
(is in his hamster imagination)
a swirling vine

climbing tiny Everests like anthills

lost coordinates in purple clouds
the green pepper awaits

a warm salamander welcome

test(i)mon(e)y

Between two WHIRLS/worlds,
sitting in a sheep pen pod
on an infernal machine wash cycle...

Synthetic fractal green tea
is simply gliding down my gullet
as my Test(i)mon(e)y begins
its 8th REAM...

DREAM - just another word
for insights into unforeseen imaginationals
breaking like waves,
breaking through the torrents of all that I have
or ever will desire.

The way back home is changing
for this wastrel/MINSTREL in tatters
and it IS the way FORWARD
to a new Dawning LOVE

that rises with every breath (breathing, breathing)
in or out it's all the SAME
and even if I take my last BREATH
my Heart will hold that one NOTE

UNTIL EVERYTHING collapses back in upon itself.

*Some say this is an ILLUSION
but i know that l-o-v-e is REAL
and the gods can still my heart forever,
they can tear it to shreds
or even SACRIFICE it upon their altars*

YET MY LOVE WILL NEVER DIE.

*Drink it in and you will find
THAT love
is ALL there is.*

music of the spherical

*the thunder drowns out
the sounds of the earth
rattling the cages along
as a volcano diverts aircraft*

*and a butterfly redirects a hurricane
while two young lovers nest in the dewy grass
entwined like two snakes lying together in union,
piercing the pre-dawn skies with cries of pleasure...*

*elsewhere, a pocketful of loose change is dropped
like pennies from heaven in a homeless woman's cup
but the donor never looks her in the eye
as they pass their go again on their way to the salon.*

*a wren cries with outrage at a loved egg
that has fallen to the ground
as a silent column of ants
queue up for a free buffet*

*not worried about the Humpty Dumpty
or how to put him back together again
because they ride for themselves
and they don't need iron horses...*

*the wind rattles the leaves of an oak
that has stood its ground for longer
than the settlers can remember
and gathers the woodpeckers into its arms*

for a round of insect morse code
tapping out Save Our Ship
to the supraterrestrial presence
listening with loving ears.

the music of the spherical
is almost imperceptible from the sleep,
the sleeping yawning vacuum that
a hapless orb suspends its hopes on.

i remember when

i remember when
the world was no bigger
than my backyard

and i would play tag
with crickets and grasshoppers
and lay upon soft grass

until daydreams
would carry me out to the edge
of where i find myself

no stone to mark my place

*my mind is variably cloudy
with a slight chance
of precipitating thoughts
this afternoon as i ponder*

*leaving this place for good
or for bad, i don't believe it matters
but the strength of the howling winds
that blow my brains out*

*tell me i soon will be tumbling
like a sagebrush across a desert stage
to who knows where, (who really cares?)
i guess i'll find out when i get there*

*or maybe not, i may just drift
or crumble in the winds and blow away
never to return to who i was
and no stone to mark my place.*

Saturday's Sojourn

*My CROWN tooth is picking up
satellite RADIO as I drive
on another MISSION*

of atmosphere REBUILDING...

*i hear "Ride, Captain, Ride"
as I MUSCLE the Jade Beast
through the DRUG traffickers.*

*I need a little more LOVE
to hang onto this FEELING
that carries ME along*

*another Joy Ride
for an Ohio Chauffeur 1951,
a very good YEAR for gears that whine*

or is that a HUM-vee?

*HARD to tell at any given moment
as Oakland may erupt in JOYOUS RIOT
at the news of Her/His arrival...*

*i make a quick EXCHANGE
for the Hi-Yo SILVER canisters
that ARE for the RELEASE workers*

*and head BACK and BEYOND
the GOLDEN mountain PASS
swiftly WAITING in the TRAFFIC preserve*

with DANGEROUS cargo.

my head

*my head pounds for pounds
longing for the solitude
(or is it solicitude?)
of a simple/single cell*

with no nucleus

*and live in sulfur steamsprings
along a lost volcanic rift
building islands
in my imagination*

*and shifting sprockets
in the clockwork universe
winding slowly down
in my consciousness...*

*the life best lived
at 7 miles per second.*

after the reflecting pool

*I got into a light quarrel
with a reflecting pool
and slipped on its mossy banks*

*as i was trying to recover
the pool's yawningness
so the children would remember*

to play keep away

*and then I found myself tumbled
in its placenta,
swirling through the warmish underwater*

*and Hey! I could breathe again
as i rose from its depths...*

*I had to rise
after all,
i had a dinner to enjoy
with a dove and a songbird*

*and I don't have to explain myself
to them
because they understand*

*Every word i remember to tell
from the Vegetable Wok dish we prepared
and set before the Three of US*

for a light snack before bedtime.

Untitled

*licorice whips into a fresnel lens to spy the peekaboo
screech owl calling nifty sluggards to the reach of
reputation a refutation of all that is twinkling on the
domelight skies of effervescent was-to-be and now it
crackles on the tweeters the hummingbird beats its wings
in cadence of a forethought the snow says spring will
amble in a bit too late for my taste to reprove the
dawning exorcism of demeter's last missed autobus and thus
making angel's snowy wings in the yards of neighing
horsehair rosined bows drawing across the violence
of terminated echo streams upon my dreams and i am but
a dew drop slipping slippers onto juliet's wristband*

The Stinker

Sitting on the Porcelain Oracle
in a s(UP!)porting role,
the backed up thoughts doth coagulate
in antici-constipation

That feels so good!

Can I s(US!)tain without
fumigating the Premises?

Highly doubtful
in this cramped crematorium...

Does a Hamster shit on its Wheel?
Only if it has the runs...

A royal flush wipes away the jeers
as I disperse my fertile fields.

time out for a wet-nap.

don't believe

*don't believe the weather here
it lies in wait for fools like me*

*the sky may be blue but my soul is orange
and the burning hills in my dreams
are soaked with the tears of many rainbows*

*don't believe the news here
it lies in wait for fools like me*

*the earth may be blue but my soul is orange
and the burning books in my dreams
are soaked with the tears of many children*

*don't believe i've had enough
it lies in wait for fools like thee*

*the life may be blue but thy soul is orange
and the burning crosses in thy dreams
are soaked with the tears of many lambs*

welcome to the jungle gym

just remember
the monkey bars can't handle
your gravitating navel
as the hands of time
slip from pole to pole

slide around
the merry-go-sound
as you scurry through the dust
to catch up with yourself
the next time you see a puffball
scanning the area
for wristwatches and quarters

someday everything
will run on quarters and hinds
drawn by the blind
seeking solace on a slip-n-glide

swingsets turn into ferous wheels
with one good to and fro
but be careful of the wraparound effect
the trapeze junkie knows
all too well
and flying without a net
was never your forty thieves
so go ahead and make a playdate
with the stars

whistle like you scream it
as the snow cone's blood drools
over the playground you have
come to call your own

until the recess bell
calls the faithful to their seats

Marsden Hartley

Vincent Gardenia may have approved
that flower in his hair
but that white shirt has no place
in a business venue especially
without a button down collar
and a pocket protector
for that fountain pen...
No, I'm sure Vincent Gardenia
wouldn't have approved of that
although I suspect he has a thing
for chest hair and pompadours.

magic poetry doodle

a careless couplet is scribbled in haste
with words of encouragement rather than waste

tendrils of meaning escaping unbroken
through magical sifting, sublime that is spoken

effortless breezes of thoughts spilling time
look easy to mages who cast spells by rhyme

extract from the innards the lyrical dances
of 'magined terpsichore in extricate chances

delicate essence drips lightly from bones
that dance in the moonlight singing with stones

hopeful love addicts will hear and yet harken
not noticing gathering clouds that skies darken

the rainbows will pierce the thunderous clouds
as worshipping rockers come gather in crowds

appearing twice nightly the pipers awaken
calling card tunes that cannot be forsaken

forever to doodle this lull-a-bye song
until words fall away from this vacuous throng

the village ideosynchrasy

*does the Hamster wear a silly hat
with a chauffer's badge attached?
of course they do...*

*tripping through the land mimes
of a small town in Bedrock Canyon
is a peace meal effort for the Village Ideo
as the counter clerics serve lattes
to impatient Borg Warners tapping morse
on clickety clackety keyboards
somewhere every day of the week.*

*Split pea lip soup warns the faithful
to keep clear heads away
from the toasted eyelid manufacturer
who wanders freely to and fro
among the faithful few.*

*next to the fulfilled Radio Shack
where wish lists doth prevail
you will find the Hamster
standing in the firing line of what
becomes a village ideosynchrasy.*

*stay tuned for what happens next
or you'll miss the previews tonight...*

another good bad day

we took the Jade Beast to the Berkeley front
and maintained a parking fine
for missing an obvious sign
two minutes into the past...

meter lady says she can't do nuthin 'bout it.

going up to the grass roots to see
about some conscious canvassing
or so we thought...

appointment's at eleven but we're early
so they put us in an empty room with some spilled dirt
and put an application in our hands...

hmm, working for the ACLU requires a background check?
seems awfully incongruous to us...

ahhh, we're not here to promote a cause
although that's the excuse posted in the want ad,
we're here to solicit contributions.

the ad said we'd make 335 to 535 dollars a week
fighting against rightwing extremism
(provided we can extract at least 100 dollars a day
or 80% of the weekly average
whichever is GREATER)

hey wait a minute, you mean the people fighting
the extremists would lie in an advertisement?
well not exactly but they kept us waiting til 11:30
and our appointment time is passed.

maybe they should post some fine print in their ads
we couldn't read anyway
so we wouldn't waste our time with such nonsense.

our time for patience has run out
and we thank the kind folks for their time and walk out.

no forwarding address

moved by mountains,
sailing along treehouse tops,
the Now defunct reject of rhyme settles for a breath.

loved by a Few,
although who knows who,
days spent wandering,
the pathways lie, as always,
to the left, center and right.

shoved into a painted word can spotlight,
tuning forked imagination to a sorcerer's spellbook,
the past left behind
traces of regret
dancing with starfish in slow motion
along the sandy shores.

proven right or wrong,
matters only dust devils worry about,
contentment never fills the empty creme inside
this twinkling Twinkie
some call Life.

an architect of wonder

playing footsie
with an architect of wonder
is a bit like receiving
without giving up your seat
in the hall of mirror
retrieval zone you created
your own damn self

namely in the first place

why should you clamor
after miracle ointments?
miracles do occur
from time to time
although you may never
get used to the feeling
an architect of wonder projects

but don't cry for l'argent-inium
while your measly worries melt away

cry hurrah! for your own architecture
you have erected as a monument
that makes others wonder
at your brilliant light

wondering (and wandering)

sitting at a Windows
sipping tea leaves through a straw hat
wondering and wandering
winding through fading memories
believing the lies the eyes tell
wishing the difference
between Heaven and Hell were less confusing
choosing a simple path to ecstatic vision
wondering and wandering

waking fruits applying apples and pomegranate
to the imagined ending
beginning to see this metaphor for what it's meaning
wondering and wandering

circling the wagons when the crows fly overhead
breaking symmetries the eye fears in the dawning Light
returning to wondering and wandering
wondering and wandering

having the moment pierce the darkening of dusk
taking a napkin by the collar
tracing the lines of a pencil drawing room
dusting off another infinite dream that only leads to
wondering and wandering
shining

the concrete vendor

*the concrete vendor is looking
to cement a new deal on a local Sherwood.
you can smell the trees just cooking
with anticipation.
parking lots are pleasing to a headlight only,
the squirrels are under reservation.*

*the concrete vendor is looking
to closeout a new millenium of hardwood.
you can smell the fires choking
with precipitation.
concrete oak trees are a bird's anomaly,
the nests will study preservation.*

*the concrete vendor is overlooking
several options that roast his dead wood.
he can only smell the green he's making
with decapitation.
cement trucks need a place to park for free,
their carcasses seek their fumed starvation.*

the bewick's wren

tiny winge'd soldier of a seed's fortune
brought down to earth by Joey Padrone

"get it out of the house!"
"do what you have to do!"

taking the wren outside in a paper towel
she looks as if she is suffering
with her feathered chest heaving

"shall i dispatch her?"
"put her out of her misery?"

looking into her eyes
the whisper returns:

"i want to live!"

can't extinguish this tiny life
put into a human's hand
tiny life that wants to live so much
she can whisper with her eyes

put her in a paper sack

"she probably won't survive the ride..."

it's 95 Fahrenheit on this Saturday
rushing to the wildlife hospital
and the directions are confusing

lost along the way
stopping for directions

*the bewick wren
is stirring in the paper sack*

"heavens, i hope she doesn't fly out the window!"

*but the winge'd soldier is injured beyond flight
flap as she may inside the paper sack*

*around the corner are the rescue workers
a safe haven lest a sparrow fall
taking her to the emergency room*

"she looks like she'll make it..."

*as the saviours take her from the paper sack
to the waiting arms of the hospital staff*

she wants to live and so she shall

fork of July (somewhere)

*it could be made into a mons stare
if we all steam an envelope in the rain showers...*

*Afterburner's at 1.234 Haught-Ashburnam was delicious tonight
last night once again as usual...*

eat a vibamin...

for your own sake...

*"Michael found one extra Lock Door spell
and is sharing it with his friends..."*

everything happened just last night i guess...

happy fork of july seekers... !!!

drop and drawl a chimpanzee loves his banana rubber ducky!!!

*erm, duckie?
liquid purple static in extra-see of lepro-cons...*

*lemurs with your tale so bright,
won't you glide my stray tonight,
er, maybe tomorrow night too...*

wash away your worries on the other side of midnight...

rain of walnuts...
peppermint flavor even,
exit,
stage through audience in a swan dive...

carry me back to old virginity...

sticks to the roof of your moth but not yer tongue groove...

sticks to the roof of your mouth but not your tongue

nothing to see here,
pick up after you leave with a sandwich,
on the house
and buy an instant lottery winner
as you exit...

casino royale flush your own toilet
port of entry with your new vaccum cleaner...

of course i'll pick up the Tabitha at the kindly garden
with a smile
that takes her back
to round at both ends and Hi! in the middle...
love you moe.

Headline tomorry

*Headline tomorry you will read expert announcement
a tactician fumbles a passed metaphor and everybody's minds
blow through everyone else's for one brief moment but it
passes quickly
many won't remember and thinktankthunk it was a dream
helpers are well ahead of schedule and cooler weather prevails
Guy Zomb(ard)-i-e plays in an elevator yesterday
in Days of Auld Lang Synergy*

*Headline tomorry you can clip the freebies in the neighbor's
refuse
where he hides his stashes and keeps locked up
but not 6 months ago so back we go
to February 14th... and don't even try
MMM, anti-venom syrup mouth-wash
trickles down to the Achille's Heel
early favorites in tomorry's primary rum-off
we're going to 1962
February 14th*

*Headline tomorry
gold certificates along the runway
offline betting odds 127,000 to 1, 12/17, a=dm geometric
action
the winner by a nose...
Earth Internet Tilt on stunning
with Rainbows in the Garden
hamsters bask in the glory of Snadragon and all behold the
fold*

*Headline tomorry
the birds are singing on a cool sundeck overlooking
fences falling in rhythmic waves like mussel turnstiles
along an Ocean bed in sublevel omicron delta 5.143*

ceasefires erupt in rapture
doors close for some and open for others
hamsters 27 running on their treadmills in orbit

Headline tomorry
love always finds a way

exeunt

exeunt all belabored atmospheric metaphors
as the clouds' weariness sets in for a cleaning cry
to wash the sticky pavements and thirsty trees,
delivering their payload especially for the soylant crop
of happy rain dancers gathered in their flocks
before the gods who strum instruments of wonder
and beat percussion caps in a rat-a-tat as if
to mow down the moshers gathered for the stage dive...

looking through droplet stained sunglasses at the spectacle,
perhaps wondering how deep the muds and flood will rise
as the muck creeps up the ankles of the revelers,
does it really matter to be swallowed whole
by the Earth's maw
and return whence the gods' repeating refrain calls you?

to be one with the mud and the flood and the song
and have the stain of love's sweetest sin at last removed
is more than you can hope for as the clouds part,
the gods cease their musical machinations
and the crowd breaks for its exeunt.

Crop Dusting

an impoverished rotational co-pilot
goes on a mission
for some improvisational crop dusting

at the Radio Shack and finds
an ultra-miniature x-ray device
from MagLite for his Chirogravitometry practice

and buys it with a used Visa gift card
from the appropriate Employee of the day...

"Nick" it says on his badge...

meanwhile...

Walking around Lafitte Circle previously
he finds the OD who can adjust his vision goggles
and the EXAM will cost 20 smackers...............

YUM, vision inspections are good for the VIEW!

walking back to the Jade Beast
he sees some Green Feather boas
just flying off the outdoor rack!

AFTER all they are MARKED DOWN!

apocalypse when?

*Lackluster reviews
have forced the eventual
cancellation of the ends
justified by the faithlessness
of sulfured paper crumbling*

*as one empire fiddles
while everywhere
its franchises burn
to the groundless accusations
of some oddly misspelled words in Aramaic*

*not necessarily leading toward any way out
of Zombie satellite view
spewing our lovesick hangover
to generations of spam-toting cybernauts
engrossed in Trivial Perplexion
over the hidden meaning of that little red button
they just noticed...*

Food? I'm hungry.

anastigmata

battle scarred
death by voice-over
i put my anastigmata on
but you won't see them
you won't know me
you won't know god(s)
offer your surrender
i may find mercy in my heart
for the dedicated warrior
i can always use a good laugh (!) @)~
the trick was taken long ago
perhaps you should try roulette
or creme de menthe
the senses are not your friends any more as far as the revealed
likes to think it has dominion over noumena

you can always try backtracking
but subliminal explosive devices must be cleared
your energy supply you hold so dear
can evaporate

Helium (the Archetype) at 3 degrees Kelvin will crawl out of
your bottlenecks and
your Large Hadron Collider doesn't scare me

can you look me in the eye
when sores cover my body?
gravity can cripple the love supply but...
Jesus wept crocodile tears
and demands for your attention are subterfuge
keep your eye on what you hold dear
as it dissolves in the (dis!)solution of mass consciousness

the appeal is denied
the repeal is denied

you have been called
POET
a report is expected on the Front Desk
but (I)nspiration is a cruel mistress
and aspiration will choke you like a clinging vine
hold steady, Inheritor!
life is dear only to those who are afraid to live it
can you stand fast
at Ground Zer0?
feel the blast?

a hero dies but once
but a poet dies with every word that she lets into her imagination
when the cloud lifts from the burning sea of glass
and all the wires scream for mercy...
when mirrors spill their foul plan
upon astonished faces looking back at WHO?
you will see me then
and if you can look beyond the scar(e)s
to ask the burning question
you may come to rest among the scriveners
who have balanced the books
but i would prefer you leave your packages with the concierge
-she has a proper gift disposal-
i have no use for the detritus of the gravity you possess
(thought deleted for lack of interest)
you should have planned your escape a little better
tunnels have been known to collapse
and mining for Truth in the depths of your soul is a dangerous profession
TRUST ME i know

*sleep will come at last to the dedicated dreamer
and those who have forgotten how to dream
will die like starfish on the sand*

living on the edge of reason(able) doubt

*something whispers doubts
into the shadows of my sunny days
so i welcome the rainy day that brings the Flood
and wash awash in the waters of the skyy*

*it's impossible to rely on lasting impressions
as everything changes so quickly
yet so persistently
and the snake can't find his tail from a blackhole in the ground.*

*everything washes away with the dregs of the skyy's drizzles
as the repentant line up for soupy nuts in convenient stacks*

EVERYWHERE

and reproducing at an alarming rate of decline.

*wishes return by popular demand in the child's eye
and the worms are tasty in the dew.*

*STANDING there like a Crucifix,
the sign where the road comes to a tee
rusts as hikers leave their business cards
in its crack.*

*i don't see any of this really happening but i'm scared
that other people do
and believe*

Iconoclast

i take down the statuary

piece by broken peace as Roman guards
cast lots for Caesar's Salad fixings under his toga...

next to Golgotha, busy workers cast fatuous glances
AT (as if) a neat row of freshly prepared Crucibles
thinking crushing a more expedient end

to a BAREfoot traveler's ministrations for the messes
left behind by lesser men than He.

OF COURSE, attaching yourself to the sticky notes of HIStory
in such a garish manor is bound to lead to no good
although the vox populi may chant and pray a name over and
over

in their fervor for further enlightenment
or simply to hold on to one more dear BREATH before
casting their Spirit to the winds of unwritten histories

In Memoriam, it is His name that is last on many dying lips
but do you suppose He cares?

or hears?

i hear although i'm not quite sure just why I CARE
when a sparrow falls

it's definitely not on purpose a game of PING PONG

*so stay DOWN if you know which way the Earth lies
to swallow your blood and tears...*

*you WILL re-emerge from this vanishing point of
breathlessness
wrought by the MANIFEST joker card
that has been placed upon your brow
by those who've held their hands folded close to their chest*

*yet all will be REVEALED
and rise you will
relishing the bitters once again*

the notorious Ms. Kraft

at first there was coffee
over some type of sales negotiations

THAT

resulted in a huge
ORDER for her and her company

and inevitably,
a large inventory of equipment

to MAINTAIN
meant more regular Visits
which we found much more productive

& Enjoyable
in a certain small motel
on the Outskirts of town.

on the first and third Friday...

I looked in her black address book once.

there were the names, addresses & phone numbers
of 25 or 30 similar motels in the Tri-State area.

that was years ago
and she was transferred a while back
but I still get excited thinking about
the first and third Friday
of EVERY month

trapezoidal

the ease with which they glide
through the air
born Maneuvers

... and no net just hard ground and sawdust ...

labored such
and falling away
as boards slide through the continuua
slicing at stray echoes
and splicing the subplot

of what the skyborn artist
feels in the center of their being...

and i am a groundling

WATCHING
imagining

hoping

my SPIRIT lifts slightly and i breathe again.

if i wake

if i wake from this dream
World inside a whorl

will you be there?

my Echo?

my Heart?

or will deathness Prevail

--the Cessation?

no, merely an intercession...

god would never permanently kill

a butterfly

maybe i didn't

maybe i didn't cause
the Ultimate Disaster after all

i'm here or seem to be
and things continue on.

where?

the keystroke strikes the chord
and the executioner does their duty

dead rat in the corner.

Oh!

when will all this failsafe deconstruct into
a tangled ball of burning yarn

and free us all...

the persistence of memory

*it's funny how each domino in History
piggybacks or dovetails on another*

*and so it is with the generations of Humankind,
and the persistence of memory
that perpetuates*

the ILLUSION

*of what follows what,
the nature of Causality*

and the Principal Arrow of Time...

footnote: it all ends at this buttjoint

Arse Poetica

with
Luke "Rapture Elk" Prater &
Robyn Dear

after Ars Poetica by Archibald Macleish

An arse should be palpable and mute
and not toot

Numb
As old toilets to the tongue

Silent as a geriatrics' home
Nut-cases, hedges where senility has grown –

An arse should be holeless
At the plight of turds

An arse should be rotational in time
As the moon climbs

Heaving, as the moon releases
Plop by plop the shite-entangled pees,

Heaving, as the moon behind the hinter grieves,
mammary by mammary the hind-

An arse should be rotational in time
As the moon climbs

An arse should be equal to:
Not poo

For all the mystery of queef
An empty toilet from a papal sheath

To shove
The leaner asses and two flights above the urea -

An arse should not dream
But be.

feel your stasis

tumbling mumbleweeds under starry skies
painted for a moment in time

an audience with the holders
of the STASH of lifting disbelief suspenders

tumbling tumbling tumbling
and sighing for rose after rose

it is the time to take the root and
cease the ceaseless murmuring of chattel ruminations

rise against the horizon-
tall, holding fast to the Earth

and feel your stasis
and let the fruits and nuts fall where they may

no room at the fall-in shelter

*a new clear freeze warning is in effect
for parts of your imagination*

during the Magnitude 2.03 birthquake.

*Vesuvius! Pay attention in class
or you'll never amount to anything.*

*equine-ox relations are at an impasse,
alert the necessary mules!*

*YOU think this game is kidding
but it's as serious as an Oreo deficiency
and the Formula,*

well, they keep changing the Formula...

*i guess i might as well
push a silver dime across a chessboard
with my nose*

teetering

*if thou wilt,
then grant me the coords to Gilead
so i can get some lip gloss*

and i'll be about my business.

existent(i)al phobia

*curiouser and strangely ordinary
to the point of
HUM DRUM
thrum thrum thrum
my heart hurts like
an Uncle Fester headlock*

*and the headlines
have their desired effect
on the Collective Psyche of the Massless*

*and now seems like it will never end
when you can't sleep
and you could fuck up a good overdose...*

NO

*rest for the Wicked/Wicker wasn't meant
to rest upon*

and I'M SCARED.

*not for myself
i've lived a good life*

*but you can't fight Natural Selection
no matter what the warning labels say*

topical euphoria

dealing with the day to day
degradations and depredations

of fairie TAIL dys(PEPTIC)utopia
collecting dream winds

to administer a topical
(or is it tropical?)
EUPHORIA

that feeling...

YES

if you can hold
yourselves together
LONG (enough) to ride the waves...

alt ending

if you can hold yourselves
TOGETHER
l-o-n-g ENOUGH to find the true wave and ride...

Your own personal Jerry
to the tune: "Your Own Personal Jesus"

Reach out and suck Face!

Your own personal Jerry
Someone who smiles
Without any guile

Your own personal Jerry
someone who smiles
who'll walk the long mile

Dreaming alone and your flesh and bone
Hunting your friends on the telephone
Lift up the receiver
He'll bring you a reliever

Fake second best
Put Love to the test
Suck on his Breast
You need to undress
He will deliver
You know he's got the fever
Reach out and suck face

Your own personal Jerry
Dreaming alone and your flesh and bone
Hunting your friends on the telephone
Lift up the receiver
He'll bring you a reliever

He will deliver
You know he's got the fever
Reach out and suck face
Your own personal Jerry
Reach out and suck face

Lamps of Self(ish) Sacrifice

We are the Lamps
Of Self(ish) Sacrifice
we turn on each other
we feast on each other's souls
ye cannot hide your Light
beneath a Bushel...

could be dangerous
for the Marshal of the Lawn Service
extinguishment services billed separately

Light your beacon for Peace
if only so you can take a moment
to take in the now...

expect miracles
why the FUCK not?

Arising Star

a twinkle
a glimmer
or is it a shimmer?

on the Horizon
on the horizontal

HOLD ME
like i shined
like i shined
like i shined

in the KOOL wind's Breath

and hence

Forth

Right

yeah right!

Basque in the glow

AFTER

Arising Star
shine(s)

a wake ending

*sitting in the back
waters of an eddy
like swirling ice
cream in a machine...*

*living the explicate,
appreciating the implicate,
and the implications*

of what each means.

*cream, they say, rises to the top
but, so too, does scum*

*and the barren barges
with propellor blades turning*

*like pinwheels
like sausage grinders*

chew the unschooled fish

like

a wake ending...

Cora Lee Brine (to the tune of Casey Jones)

Drivin' through Rain
High on Romaine
Tasty tunes are playin'
In my head

Double the Dead
Double the Time
And you know the Ocean
Looks like Wine

This old Toyota
Makes me feel fine
Leaves my garage about any old time

Radio sleepin'
Freak 1-0 point 2
Wakes up again just a hummin' a tune

Driving through Rain
High on Romaine
Tasty tunes are playin'
Hear the Dead

Double the Bread
Double the Time
And you know the Ocean
Feels just fine

Snorkels are ready
I'm feelin' sublime
Takin' a tour through a Cora Lee Brine

Purple Fish dartin'
With Laughter for Dead
Run through my fingers like the hair on my head

Drivin' through Rain
High on Romaine
Tasty tunes are playin'
In my Head

Double the Dead
Double the Time
And you know my Ocean
Tastes like Wine

And you know my Ocean
ta-astes like wi-i-ine

Written for Japa Kaur's Birthday

a twist of simple Faith

to believe
or weave fables of broken myth
the mythos is the key
to unlocking the Word

with a twist of simple Faith

to delve
into worlds inside untapped
and believe
against the buffeting currents of disbelief

employing a twist of simple Faith

to dwell
where beacons shine their Light
and see
the shore approach
not to encroach upon the founder's rock

and trust your twist of simple Faith

At Play in the Fields of the Hive Ward

Doing a Thorazine shuffle

At PLAY
in the fields of the Hive Ward

Here comes Dora the Exploratory
in HIS Red Silk Kimono Pink Tutu & Blue Leg(ging)5

He she nods and needs to know
He is a She
and was mis-assigned/misaligned

Kevin handles the 13EA577 in his sleep
and fondles my M & M's
with his butthole probing fingers

gotta learn to live with it

At PLAY
in the fields of the Hive Ward

Janette orders Butalbital in the Mail
and eats it like Red Hot candies

OH GOD
ECT TOMORROW
!?

It's time for Medication so we line up

Like CATTLE
Like Chattel

At PLAY
in the fields of the Hive Ward

Hospital DINNER is served
WE eat and Mumble funny stuff to each other

On a Galaxy Quest
It's Tuesday,
it's Movie night.
We gather in the Cloud Chamber.

Four Fingered Gus is Strummin'
Good Times

We all sing a song
At PLAY

in the fields of the Hive Ward

Hiyo Bastards! (the Dukes of Biohazzard)

Bastard stepchildren twice removed
Dawdling at the four front toothy grinmobiles
Hillside dangling like rapelling spiders

Gotta take the Still
Gotta burn the Rope

Hiyo Bastards!
This is my piece of Land...
This is my Burial Ground...
The Cemetery Plot thickens for my Bones

But they ain't ready.

Time and Circumstance
Forces the Dukes' hands
To Soil the Till once again...

A modicum of Silver Beans
To buy the COW

Hiyo Bastards!
This is my piece of Land...
This is my Burial Ground...
The Cemetery Plot thickens for my Bones

But they ain't ready.

You ain't the Poor White Trash
Your Father WAS
You have a decent Edu(Ma)Cation

So to Speak
Speak only when Spoken to

Hiyo Bastards!
This is my piece of Land...
This is my Burial Ground...
The Cemetery Plot thickens for my Bones

But they ain't ready.

If the Dukes think it's Funny
It'll sell out like a Cell Out
And the margins recede as they are called

Many are Chosen
But FEW are Ready...

Hiyo Bastards!
This is my piece of Land...
This is my Burial Ground...
The Cemetery Plot thickens for my Bones

But they ain't ready, YET

yet...

Shocking Pink Dandelions

Great big bunches of Shocking Pink Dandelions
Fill the Limelight Fields across the Valley
Drinking as Freely from the Moonbeam Drops
As they do the Sun's

Like Neon Flashbulbs under Full Moon skies
I hear their cries
Of Joy for Silver Silence
On a Night of Spring Wonderment
As I descend to lie among them

To Channel the almost imperceptible
Dream Frequencies they emit
I catch new episodes
Of I Love Lucy in the Sky
And dare not wonder why
As I lay my body on the dewy fields among them

They sing me a Lullaby
Garnished with Lollipop Somniferum
And the Dream begins to quietly unfold
As I drift off to join
The Shocking Pink Dandelions
In the Land of Their Dreams

underestimated prophet

*speaking in parabolic mirror images
forked tongue flicking in and out
of black lips pursed to whistle Dixie*

*banging a tin cup against the rail
at the station holding a banjo case
and muttering false fallacies at the passersby*

*he's been walking the streets for years
preaching the end is near
and at least for him*

*at least for him
grabbing a candy bar off a bench
looks like a slice of Paradise*

Bless the Lord for Providence

*If nobody looks him in the eyes
If nobody hears the wisdom of the street
If nobody stops to hear his story*

*is it because
is it because he is an underestimated prophet
cast aside by society's glances*

*too far gone to be dusted off and polished
too near the throne of the Lamb
for the fearful to approach*

*as he lays on a bench to meet the Lord again
if only in his dreams*

Humpty Dumpty

Humpty Dumpty had a Great Wish
He desired to catch a Great Big Fish
He sat in his boat with his rod and reel
Soon a Gigantus took a snatch by the feel
He wrestled and wrangled but all to no good
Gigantus pulled back and ate Humpty for Food

the lingering donuts

i ate six
six
count them
six
raspberry filled donuts

and they
are lingering
in my belly

like a bag of cement products

and you can't expect
a leopard hamster
to connect its freaking dots

with a belly full
of six
six
count them
six
raspberry filled donuts

lingering
dawdling in the doldrums
of my bowels

what do you suppose will come out of all this?

i am the dust

i am the dust
filling the tombs of forgotten lovers
muting the hearts of those they've left behind

ghostly lovers reuniting under the Earth
mingling like the dust they have become
no vision
the only promise

Poems Written in Ohio
After July 1, 2011

The L(e)ast Bastion

Standing like an evergreen
On a forgotten hill
The morning star rises
Greeting the lost lovers

Lost but not forsaken
In here
The L(e)ast Bastion left
Against the buffeting winds of stillborn Fate

High upon the crosscurrents of immortality
Ratcheting the last turns of the screw you
Unforgiving world

You have your L(e)ast Bastion
With your cake and eat it too
Too much for the hard soul to swallow

And gently into that good morn you go.

Leaving Paradise

Eden is beautiful to the unwary eye
but danger ever lurks in this quiet garden.
The fruit hangs all about,
the branches bending low,
we laugh and run to the edges of cool content
but the serpents twine the shiny fruit.

What danger lurks in this quiet garden?
The danger that our eyes will open
and see each other for who we really are,
not the playful lovers caught in sweet embrace
but two more vipers seeking shelter from the eyes
of each other, the gods we have chosen to be.

To be innocent of wisdom's stain
and hear the Garden's sweet refrain
is still our sweetest desire
but knowing that we are not
the children we pretend to be
makes bitter every shining globe we pluck.

Circumstance has opened our eyes
as we coil our tails like the Cadduceus.
I am not a carefree lad
and you are not an innocent maid,
we have made our bed a nest
of haunting lies, of haunting lies.

We could start over somewhere else
but would we find more bitter fruit
or grapes of wrath upon the vine?
Time will tell this twisted tale
woven with the secrets we have kept,
but we must try, we must try.

*We are still two vipers
and leaving the Garden behind,
what will we find, what will we find?
That we have grown in each other's eyes?
Or will there be no room for love
upon this new and darkling plain.*

*I am certain of this one thing
that even two serpents can find embrace
and there must be fruit that we can share
that has a sweeter taste.*

The Kill Switch

it is the last sacrifice of a mortal
coiled like a serpent
ready to strike
with remote control

passed like a servant of solitude
passed like a stone through a catheter

waiting for the moment
perhaps a last breath
perhaps a second chance where there is none

what do you say
to this last lunge of the kill switch
as life drains from your veins?

what do you think?
will the consequence of your failures
bring the desired result?

passed like a servant of solitude
passed like a rainbow through the eye of a needle

waiting

for one last flip of the switch

Man of la Munchies

emerging from a cloudy haze
upon a grassy knowl-
edge

the dealy lama applauds silently

he takes his magic staff and tilts
at the golden arches
for burgers on demand

except

he does not partake of the flesh
of brother-cousin-cow

you want some fries with that shaky hand?

battered (like a ram's breath)

he thinks not
so he tilts
on full-tilt

at two golden arches
sickened
by the smell of flesh

stick a saddle on a moonbeam

*the throng stands hushed
against the cold rain
against the cold rain*

*you and i hold each other close
under an umbrella*

*we are only spectators
we are only spectral*

*they hold signs and beat drums
against the cold rain
against the cold rain*

*you and i hold each other's promises
as though the throng is ours*

*we are in a moment of time
we are watching the world change*

*a megaphone blares out
against the cold rain
against the cold rain*

*you and i listen to each other's hearts beat
differentiated from the throng*

*we are only lovers
we are only the promise*

*everywhere we turn
everywhere we look
people are awakening*

and yet
love never changes

so what are we to do in this sea of changes?
as the rain gives way and the throng begins to stir?

stick a saddle on a moonbeam
and never ever forget to dream

freaks be free

*break out of your corrugated cardboard boxes
and open your petals to the metallic sun,
shout obscenities at stop signs for a laugh.*

*twist away the night with weirdlings in open spaces
under careless debris falling from the sky,
it's only satellite junk, it means no harm
and what are the odds?*

*stand in a circle and beat drums and kazoo symphonies,
time is a thief destined to take away guarded smiles.*

*laugh like you mean it even showered by pellets,
the heavy can't wash away unpainted smiles.
let them wonder where their Santa suits belong
toting their artillery to no effect.*

*wear your bleeding hearts on your sleeves
or ink them into your skin,
there's no sin in showing where your head is at.*

*leave empty suits standing
with their mouths gathering flies
as you dance among the pylons
keeping you out and keeping them in,
you are impervious to the diatribes of the sadly normal.*

*above all know that when you are who you really are
you are really free and no one,
no one can take that away from you*

*so let them wonder why you're smiling,
the heavy always sink to the bottom,
it's a universal law.*

*and when they cart away the sticks and stones
you'll know it,
you'll know it by the smell of dead men's bones
and be satisfied that the imperative of the freaks
(and that's what you are)
the imperative is to be free above all else.*

spare some change

wish i had a drink right now...

seems like a good spot,
30,000 people crowded into a small square,
they got tents and heaters and oh God! all that food.

i get my plastic cup and sign out of my shopping cart
(i di'n't steal it, a friend gave it to me, yeah)

it's cold out here and i wish i had a drink right now...

"can you spare some change?" i say to the empty suit
trying so hard not to look my way,
you never know, once one of these empty suits
dropped a twenty in my cup.

i remember back before i lived under the overpass,
a long time ago, or so it seems,
on some goddamned desert, tanks burning in the sun,
we took a grenade and i shit my pants.

i'd shit my pants right now for a drink...

lots of signs being carried round this place,
will anybody see mine?
a bottle of wine is only $3.68 with tax
and i have a $1.42
but the Lord will provide.

that long-haired man has a five in his hand,
don't look him in the eye,
don't look him in the eye.

he doesn't see me and walks past.

a couple quarters from some sweet young thing!
i didn't even see her,
don't look her in the eye,
don't look her in the eye.

"thank you!" i mumble.

i'll just push my cart to where the food is,
maybe somebody will see my sign,

God, i need a drink...

some young dude leaves a sandwich at my feet,
i knew it, the Lord does provide.

in high school, i was voted class optimist,
it serves me well right now, just about right now.

some odd change and a couple ones from a kind soul.
"buy yourself something to eat" they say.
don't look them in the eye,
don't look them in the eye.

"thanks!" ("don't tell me how to spend my money!" i think to myself)

there's a liquor store near the overpass,
i can go back home to my warm spot with my bottle
(if the cops haven't taken down my boxes)
things don't change much under the overpass.

i push my little world on up the street.
the Lord will provide, it's a good day to be alive.

leaving earth

in a dream
my spirit flies
far above the earth

i see

a vista of what
is to (be)come
of me
of us

in pools rising
like swirls of RNA
and glittering
with colors no eye has seen

&

i follow
this flowing stream
among the filaments of consciousness

out to the edges
out to the EDGE

and glow like they do
in the silence of space
taking up new color

reacting to the expanses
of inner solitude
i am but a winding string
longing to unwind
and merge

but i remain separated
for what reason i do not know

but follow
the overcurrent back in TIME

to home
my home
our home

and awaken to find
i am alone

what mary meant

what mary meant when she said

WHEN SHE SAID

let go of yourself to find yourself and you WILL find yourself
i wonder now as i ride the rail back east

what mary meant when she said

WHEN SHE SAID

to master the moment you must be in the moment
i wonder now as i sit in the lap of urban disease

what mary meant when she said

WHEN SHE SAID

you can catch more lies with vinegar
i wonder now as i drift off in an alcoholic haze

mary says a lot of things not all of which she means
so maybe she was just shooting the shit
or maybe not

i am a bird

i am a bird
alone
in a gilded cage

with no other bird
to sing to me
or teach me her songs

through the window
in the distance
i hear the other birds

and their melodies
and their songs
of joy
and of sorrow

though i seldom remember
their words

i don't know
what bird i am
nor do i care

i sing the one song
i know

i am a bird
alone
in a gilded cage

how i learned to ignore the ticking and love the bomb

tick tock

sitting on a powder keg
of disaffected and disenfranchised

youth has not had its way

the Plutarch lives and moves
in Darkness

dead men's bone(r)s rattle around
the marketplace

i have a picture of it in my wallet
not much else in it

i like buttons for some strange reason
so i wear them on my clothes and hats

buttons likes me

next to Jupiter
they say there's a water satellite
whatever that means

a swan dive into infinity at any moment
at any moment

every Breath is a Gift

and i expect an early landing somewheres

tick tock

Made in the USA
Charleston, SC
21 January 2012